Pin Up Girls

COLORING BOOK

tilda mallin

Pin Up Girls Coloring Book for Adults

Copyright © Tilda Mallin

First published 2023

ISBN 9798372679603

Edited and typeset by Tilda Mallin

Cover design by Tilda Mallin

Thank you for showing your support. We would be very pleased to hear from you. Please scan the QR Code to leave a review.

Amazon USA

Amazon Canada

THIS BOOK BELONGS TO

"

"

COLOR TEST PAGE

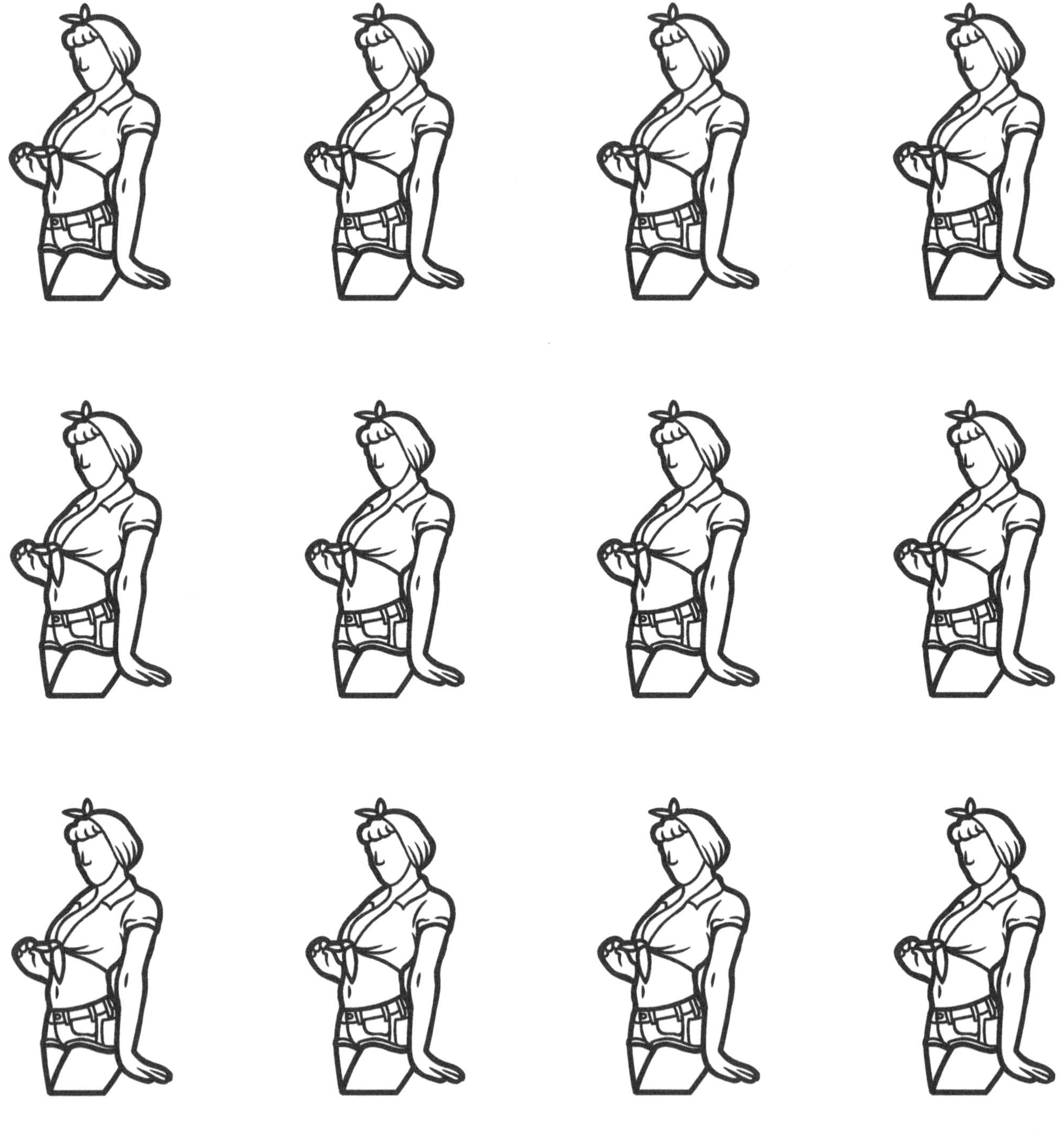

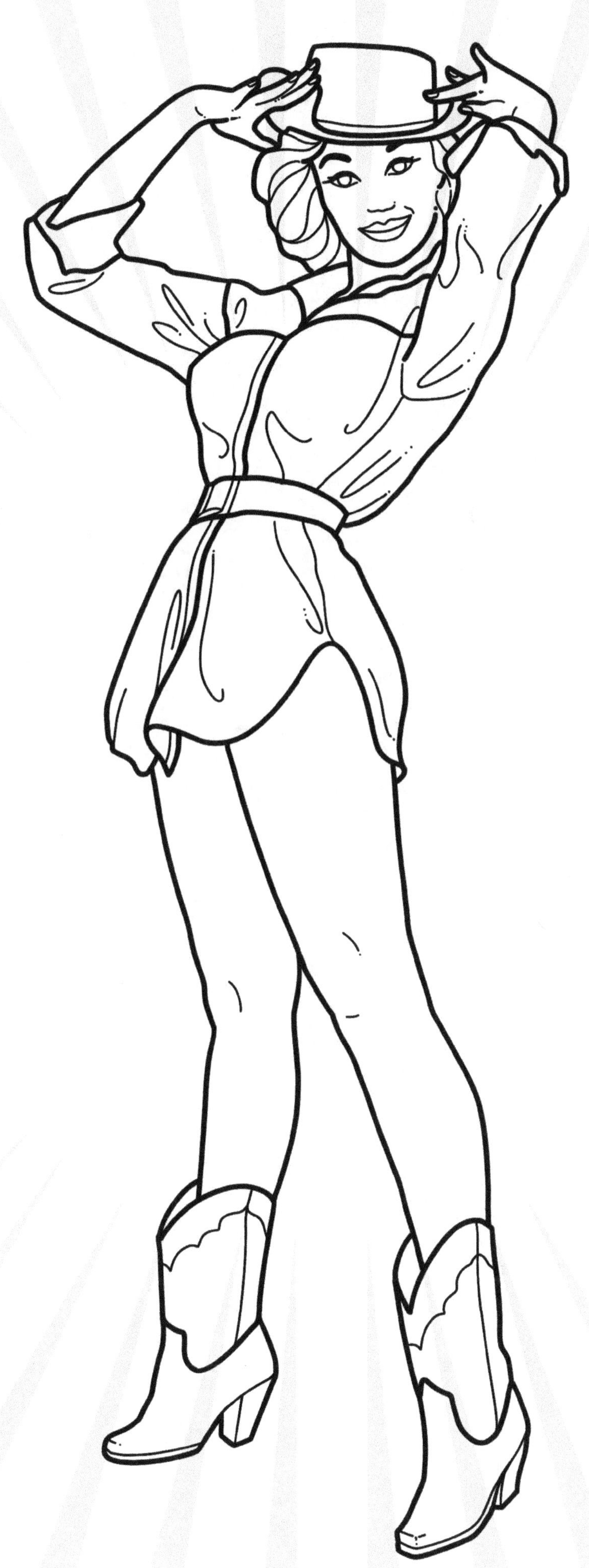

HOW TO
BE A
WELDER

www.ingramcontent.com/pod-product-compliance
Lightning Source LLC
Chambersburg PA
CBHW081810250726
48653CB00010B/3877